Halve

**The Tupelo Press First / Second Book Award:
The Berkshire Prize**

Jennifer Michael Hecht, *The Last Ancient World*
    Selected by Janet Holmes

Aimee Nezhukumatathil, *Miracle Fruit*
    Selected by Gregory Orr

Bill Van Every, *Devoted Creatures*
    Selected by Thomas Lux

David Petruzelli, *Everyone Coming Toward You*
    Selected by Campbell McGrath

Lillias Bever, *Bellini in Istanbul*
    Selected by Michael Collier

Dwaine Rieves, *When the Eye Forms*
    Selected by Carolyn Forché

Kristin Bock, *Cloisters*
    Selected by David St. John

Jennifer Militello, *Flinch of Song*
    Selected by Carol Ann Davis and Jeffrey Levine

Megan Snyder-Camp, *The Forest of Sure Things*
    Selected by Carol Ann Davis and Jeffrey Levine

Daniel Khalastchi, *Manoleria*
    Selected by Carol Ann Davis and Jeffrey Levine

Mary Molinary, *Mary & the Giant Mechanism*
    Selected by Carol Ann Davis and Jeffrey Levine

Ye Chun, *Lantern Puzzle*
    Selected by D. A. Powell

Kristina Jipson, *Halve*
    Selected by Dan Beachy-Quick

HALVE

Kristina Jipson

POEMS

Tupelo Press
North Adams, Massachusetts

Halve.
Copyright © 2016 Kristina Jipson All rights reserved.

Library of Congress Cataloging-in-Publication Data

Names: Jipson, Kristina, 1981- author.
Title: Halve : poems / Kristina Jipson.
Description: North Adams, Massachusetts : Tupelo Press, 2016. | Series: The Tupelo Press First / Second Book Award | Includes bibliographical references. | The Berkshire Prize.
Identifiers: LCCN 2016001117 | ISBN 9781936797714 (pbk. : alk. paper)
Subjects: LCSH: Grief--Poetry.
Classification: LCC PS3610.I67 A6 2016 | DDC 811/.6--dc23

Cover and text designed by Bill Kuch.
Cover photograph: "Daydream," by Richard Cofrancesco.
Used with permission of the photographer. http://www.racfocus.com

First paperback edition: March 2016.

Other than brief excerpts for reviews and commentaries, no part of this book may be reproduced by any means without permission of the publisher. Please address requests for reprint permission or for course-adoption discounts to:

Tupelo Press
P.O. Box 1767, North Adams, Massachusetts 01247
Telephone: (413) 664–9611 / editor@tupelopress.org / www.tupelopress.org

Tupelo Press is an award-winning independent literary press that publishes fine fiction, nonfiction, and poetry in books that are a joy to hold as well as read. Tupelo Press is a registered 501(c)(3) nonprofit organization, and we rely on public support to carry out our mission of publishing extraordinary work that may be outside the realm of the large commercial publishers. Financial donations are welcome and are tax deductible.

For my brother, Travis. This book was written with the memory of our childhood together held near.

CONTENTS

Like Lamps along the Shoreline
1

Lock, Means
9

Limbs Move Wind In
19

But We Meant I Did
35

Lock, Means
45

Green State
55

Notes
69

Acknowledgments
70

*As transparent bodies suffer
light to pass through them,
retouching greens the trees*

*visible through the glass with
bursts of fill-in flashes to lift
the shadows. Perhaps*

*his hair was dark and it was
sun cast on it that made him
seem blond. A vision*

*she says but it was wrong to ask
for messages we didn't want. I
would not let him in. Come*

*unexceptional this to tell us
now we are here and little
more definite as visions*

*than as bodies limply passing
through denser mediums to empty
these rooms of every sound.*

.

Like Lamps along the Shoreline

will says I would do or we are part of this
begins with resolves to actually watch this time

as it happens like this that we mark periods of time
in quality of experience or say it wasn't a seeing

of the black wick burnt against the glass like summers
at the end of the wharf where his hair was a passing

to the lake went brown that time of day and we went all
brown or I the sort of person to make

that sort of story mean we will have having for one
another only with this second

awareness that our surroundings double
to offer something other

we do not name as it draws visual
the periphery and scarcely sometimes

what he said I'd miss is present as a thickness or
his hand on mine for a moment presses

the pines into wedges in the distance
where I tried evenings alone in the grass sharp with cold

forgetting what recedes from vivid to all
those nights were a sparkler made a brightening made

bright arcs out of brown off the lake and his hair
was infinitely little parts parting themselves at the end

of the wharf where change was already taking
place apart from meaning or those summers apart

from we imagined now to mean we would not lose him
though we lost him and now allow the lapses longer

motions through the brown to make a sort or sense
from the wasness of he stood in that way and the thrill

a way of not saying how to say no
matter what I say there are times I have

no choice but to respond if only now and not
all through me to an excitation

like an imaging of itself in the all-brown
of our movement together toward the water

where suddenly between us there is room
for the rooms where our motion makes the lake

Lock, Means

This is the pattern: porch, stairs, grass up from under. And always light
as if from lamps along the shoreline. Aim, explicit, is a problem conception
makes. He stood beside the house with his arms stretched wide

to fall. Pattern mandates. We are not similar in our selves—there is no similarity prior to response. I see many, many-sized. Rings in

Marigolds, the Door

        Cling leaves our hands to the floor,
            is a light shape

on the hardwood, is the bedspread
    unfinished, is we

        rouse him. I remember starting
            is droning, is advect

yard to field and we waive him. So
    we bother. Turn faces

        to plural so we are him. Bring
            is the bedroom

colored late day, is the bedroom,
    is our hurt him.

        We would rouse him. Is the hallway,
            dims the hallway

where we bother because we bother.
    We put clothes on,

        which is comb through. We grow
            damp where we

heat through. It is soft where we slow
    to stop touching.

        I am obvious—let me say this—
            it's humiliating.

I remember that it feathered, is we
    hearten or we

        love for. We feel close to close wrists
            in the hallway—

the drawer. This connected, the setting varies, as in porchside was creekside was the sound of his feet in the gravel by the roadside. Pattern is possession, is a process of revealing

Drawer, in Hopes

Not ghostly,
        tied like that. Is collect them.
Still weight
        at the top of the stairs and it isn't.
Or approach
        us. We arrange them. Still they
come for.
        Rise is his face or our faces, is we
wait for, is agreed
        we do not leave the house. It wants
patience to
        endure it, but I have it. Is can
multiply, then
        reduce it. I believed before
despite we—
        was a wanting, is our mouths turn
and we mean
        to make a home. We collect
them for it. Still
        no denser, though we shut what
shuts, though I say
        sometimes, to him, I miss it
as we look for.

what's already there. I imagined horses; he probably imagined something else. Windowed apart from action—mine through glass from different places. Arrange is measure, a means for maintaining congruity of favor between us. Let me. An outline—no, a reordering. Pattern replicates; it transposes. We can let principle inform the layering, make a middle of our wanting to remember together. This is only one way of saying. Look, I made these for him—I stood in the yard and the trees were rings and rings

Limbs Move
Wind In

light compressed to plaid faces
turns the water where the water

makes lines in his face in small colors
called halves. Our failure

to appreciate the correspondence
between our two rooms made

all the more striking the fact we were told
explicitly about it. Shape makes subtle

gestures revealing attachment: the shrinking
of boundaries, also of distance,

With palms above our fingers
grasping we lift many times
the small box, weighted
for release. Overlapping black
obscures much of what's behind
this movement broadly projected
toward the observer as if conducted
in recognizable space. The stick-
house appears as from the front
yard: one set of nearly horizontal

lines converges at its right; another
runs the front-facing planes
of the house and porch to the left.
There are four window boxes;
the windows above them appear
wedgelike. Edges imitate visual
rays; we can use traces to position
our imaginary eye level devotionally
below him where he observes, though
we may actually stand above him.

and through that unfamiliar
medium touched responding
places in the room itself.

With palms above our
fingers grasping we drew
many times the water

upward from the water
where threads of black between-
matter made the afternoon

wet light through our
hands to bent rows
of pressure on the floorboards.

a more intense scrutiny of human
features. He understood about

pictures. They are maps that give away
hiding places. I searched

hard for him
but didn't realize I had been given

any way of knowing where
he was. His hand

puppeted shadows on a surface barely
visible a hiding event, one sort

These days of the winter half
months have neither the names
nor dates of weekdays. We push
thumbs against the area between
the house and its relief where
fading continuity creates
irresolvable ambiguities. Our
tender manipulation of the sticks
opens small spaces in
this plane others could also

occupy. We turn the house;
the front porch appears nearer
than the back stoop, and the stairs
appear identically sized. Fingers
clasped, we play at introducing
occlusion—imagine outer
walls opaque. This is a planting
of red in the window boxes,
a repositioning of the vanishing
point beyond each nearby exit.

If transparent, our perspective,
the water was a measure—
summer a side of an opposite

push away from the middle,
this the other way of growing
smaller the season

of indoor effects. We turned
faces to face how closely
we set our fingers, grasping

under the low light and the lamp
was a cold bulb turned
forward to forced bloom

of illumination. We knew about
the symbolic potential of given details—

arranged them into several sorts
of sequences. The duplicate space

shuttered. He hung the cut-out pictures
from strings in the spare room.

Proportion crept in; things that were
greater or much smaller than the objects

we were accustomed to altered
the space, made our world

Or just behind his far right
temple where he stands
on the lawn with his making
fingers; in this house nearby
exits are also distant entrances.
The house is a triangle;
tracing its narrow to its wide
takes longer than expected. We push
one-sided images into solid as if
the real-world horizon were pictured

in the flat; we force in qualities
of ordinary space. Widening
the hole captures more rays
but the images grow too blurred
to be useful. The floor appears
as underground and the stones
of the walk as paper-thin moons
in the paper. Anything he finds
he finds to be his in this construction
still holding its own on the table.

contained in the yard
where we stood in the yard
making finger shapes

into threads of black water
like lines. Sudden illumination
opened through any point

dark colors that dispersed
into our grasping an under-
the-water as a surface

of shades etched weaker
our division, reluctant
into three—

more livable. Two representations
were active at once; images traced

through the pictures were visible
in reverse on the opposite side.

There were connections between stages
of incompletion. Our afternoon remained

unfinished—the bedroom wall
unpainted. Unexpected

relationships formed between
marginal pictures and our favorite things—

Vaguely, one of two divisions
more or less approaching
equality. Limit to halve what
pieces are found by another.
We do—imperfectly—in order
to present ourselves simply.
Each surface hides an opposition
another reveals, and reveals
fracture when necessary. In
numbers the half holds the same

proportion to the whole as in
objects, but all connection
with space is lost. We refuse
to believe we are figures. He
brings his fingers with equal
pressure against either side
of our house, and the pressure
makes his fingers potentially
unlimited bodies lifting the house
toward its margins, accelerated.

Our palms were black
backgrounds against the water
in the yard where the water

grew from underground
to that horizon drawn
past the end of focusing

on our palms lifted and so
large when inverted
they obscured everything

in the room. We traced
rays from corner to corner
to indicate in the darkness

that we felt blackened
on the inside we figures
occupying spaces

others should also occupy
and our grasping
was mesmerizing because of it.

his hand revolved a wheel that mixed
colors we took to be papers.

He knew that hole was made
by a nail. We peeled back the yellow

wrapper to reveal a minutely finished
production of the room in which

we stood. He knew how to find
me, drawn small

within the frame—spectacular
those heavy lines that marked

the water with long periods
of unornamented inactivity.

But We Meant I Did

It's colder here beside the window where I can see

two black edges, the lamp digging wings

from the wall. The quilt drawn flat makes deep

creases where our bodies were, turning. I remember

the hardwood was yellow hair where we stood

hand-colored and dressing for school. There are rules

for feeling better, little breath noises. It takes seven

pauses to go from the roofline to the lake; one is

owl sounds in the heat, another is how owls sound

like sirens far away. Also, his thigh underwater.

If it's there, why look for it, she said. We thought

birches had an odor, and that snow did. I could

make the lampshade round like it was; I could make

black circles on the red. Said, it takes longer to imagine

than to say. The lake was bright gray cubes pressing cold

past his knees. We waited all night in the hallway—that was how

we learned we could make something there by saying

it wasn't. I don't know what changed, she said—

our winter collapsed into a series of single instants punctuated

by a white stripe drawn from the sky to our fingers

thrown out against the wind. And here, that same white

between the birches eclipses the subject, which must be us.

What we meant was, pay attention to us. In the same way

I want to say something about what it's like in this corner

and how I want it otherwise. Or that this means

getting farther from how it happened. We posed

with our arms touching exactly in the center of the frame

as if we didn't know the light would leak there. She said

we were safe, but the boat beat hard against the green

between the canyon walls, and the pots fell from their hooks

to the linoleum. Walking the other way was not a solution.

I remember our voices as if from above the roofline, forcing

shadows onto the grass where we with a mania for that

exact temperature in the dark ran circles around our legs

and called it winning. Neither was being loud about it. It was a way

of holding our time together apart from the hum of the house with its blinds drawn down inside the night. And a way of saving for later

that overhead feeling. We thought we knew what the sky looked like

and how we looked through it—mostly blue-black, and very fast.

His pasting of the sticks more firmly together was an act of devotion,

though he lied about it. It turned out perfectly, she said, turning

the tray in slow circles on the table. And it was true, if you looked

long enough, the scene did appear bigger from above, just as his room

felt different after he was gone. We never thought our house

might be identical to the others in those miles of subdivisions

that lined the freeway with its signs we believed marked

places like ours: the lemon tree, the two ropes, the cold between

the hills. Lower voices meant they were saying important things and him in the bathroom meant those kids making fun

of his socks. These are just sketches, he said, his hair making bright

rings above his ears. Attention means a lot: how our wanting

something strange to happen made edges of the lights

at the tip of the airplane's wing, plastic sounds

as we opened our books from the library. She paused before she said,

of course I loved him. And I am a little worse again but at least this time

I know why. It's impossible to get back to how it seemed even

days ago—it's as if this room would rather not. The proof is how

this no longer feels like anything. I'm not angry,

she said, I'm disappointed. Still, we tried everything to fix it.

Yes, this mess is a way of saying we are resigned here

to sleeping at odd times through the day. We called it a river

but it was a ditch, drying even as we watched it. We thought

they refused to believe because we did. We pressed

our palms into the dust to wash them and we trusted it

to work. I knew the lamp made the colors on the ceiling like a map

and time from outside would ruin it. That was sleeping

when it was hard to. Or how adults in our memories stayed

the same age. We could close the door when we wanted

but the window persisted: crickets, the field,

how it got hotter out loud. It's only a tragedy if it happens

to you, she said. My belief that he will come back

is what woke me. And the corner grows to brown

shoulders where our clothes go over in mounds. Let them

leave then, she said. And, that's how it is. We hid

our eggs under the grass in our baskets to trick them

but it didn't. Those of us who wished to change were frustrated,

then saddened. Yes, it was nice the way he said, remember me

to them, but we forgot. And he sat all day on the porch

because he could smoke there. Really, it was a way for us to explain

things to ourselves. When they said, imagine, all I could see

was a corner lit by a lamppost made of a pencil,

which made me think there was something wrong with me.

We were always aware of the potential for crisis—

it was threads in the body, pulled down. Or before:

brown knives of grass in the yard behind the house.

Anyone could see you there, she said. As now is built

of thin, pale blue made of white and a bowl

beside the window, full of marbles. Whatever is here will fit

and is enough, she said—just as the air was early

winter if you crouched down low beside the fence

dividing us from the neighbors' where the kids stayed

up all night. Now this bed looks just like a bed, like I was

never here at all. Put those down anywhere, she said:

the box spilled lit threads under the bulb in the basement.

Lock, Means

Pattern is repetition—qualities multiply felt in a field of instances marked by convergent responses. Our talk is small but is a semblance, is our ambit, is sometimes I see lines in things as if he sketched them. The dot coincides with the line, or displaces it. Pattern yields direction—

a manner and a method, which is stillness into asking, or is asking into stop. It was not conceit—that drawn feeling—it told. Pattern admits instances not as actual instances but as conditions for potential instances. It was hot in the sun where I sat

Has a Blue Tint

      Where the hall falls beside
in the would-light,
           in the were

      we, in our small grown nudging
at the was once.
         Soothe me;

      it matters. Was the sunlight
or our blink for—we
         held hands

      and were hold for. Or the sun
through the door was
         a black spot,

      was the sunlight, was his back
where he stooped and
         it meant it

      changes to diminish. Talk
is his hand apathetic, is
         our room for,

      is would mouth it. I would
bite it. In this room for
         I can see it—

      it sharpens. We abridge. All
over the hills are cut with
         small waters.

calling him. The sequence was discernable, if reversed; his voice over distance as the contrast defining the scope of the lapses between moments, collected. I cannot tell him—

Pair As, Took Hands

                to hold, vaguely. It in parts:
      before, it was a lit-ness, was a way to,

was our giving in to work through
      in versions. It wears us. We do

            with boughs that are windows
what this draft does with seasons—

very little. We repeat.
      It makes volume

           where we sleep more, which is ringing
when we wake more to find

one on each side of each of our bodies,
      disposing. We need our share

           in the doing of something. His is
practice, is cast us, is burden

our arms beyond their wrists
      which restrain us. He

           reams in phases what we don't
say to stay us—the chairs

where we dry in the chill with our hands
      on our hands and our mouths

           in hard grooves as the field
bears rows over brushstrokes. We are

margined, then to liven. We were
      so pretty there. If

           culled—so many
through whom we were passing.

I remember, but not well. Pattern is a tendency upon which the prediction of subsequent events may be based. We pulled the shade down. At length I force myself into the bathroom and I open the taps. Nor was that it.

Box, Beside

                Please trains our ears
to the door in the dark
       where our twice more tries

our tried for into
       yarn unthreading the carpet

            or we in twos doing voices
again: I to you to plead
       him down from the roof

              where bright holes bored from blue
       make it darker. We there

              holding remains the same as
sameness staying the curtains to map whole
       plots across the wall (the lamp

            beside the bed;
       the light beside

       the bed) or one to bind
the door to through and more
       to force to still all those things

            we must have
       thought: that we weigh what I strain

            to let through that light
beside the bed to burn to one those
       two who sit you

            up all night to tell you this:
       that he staked upright in that light

>   beside the bed with the door shut fast
> doesn't live here anymore. To say to you
>   as one to one in the dark

>   who else would sit you up
>   all night and tell you this.

Green State

Our identical words might constitute two
        ways of framing: ours,
the pines seen round the outside so near
        together in their action
against the dark; ours, our similar parts
        left together in that room
ringed by its distance from the pines.
        We would make good
pictures of our sometimes accidental searches
        as we would make good

of what is faint or dark in the pictures. Hands,
        the pines, cracks less visible
in the wood than in bright arcs radiating
        white over the glass. We shut
out by effort our awareness of what little
        variation in light that room gave
to cue us and watched the white to white
        passing as intensification
suggesting collection, a mounting on itself
        the contents of that sky

separating us from the rim. Our nearly touching
    features, no less objects
than drawn splashes across that sky, waxed
    damp in their resisting
the over-whiteness as water resists submergence
    within itself. The pines
as the glass supported around us fully or partially
    submerged us into a flux
so constant as to allow no difference to pierce
    those walls we thought permeable.

The frame: our static postures there behind
    the glass choosing not one
course over another but one course after another
    in succession like the thickening
of our exhalations slowly raising a descending
    force against the house.
But we could move our bodies. We could
    choose whether and how much
to be immersed. There only through our
    deliberate seeing as: hands, the pines,

that room for our coming slowly to consider
    what it is we may have wanted
to ask. Whether if we could not find
    sensible-sounding sounds
with which to describe our experiences we must
    feel in our embarrassed way
our experiences to be beyond the range
    of sensible. Our making
impulse was to realize, to make back from
    our realizations the pines

acting blackly around the house to give us
    far off even in our wondering
at our strikes against the white to prove
    their darkness was an edge.
It was too many ways at once. We to start
    would agree to start, which was
less than how to do it. We could imagine well
    motions more intimate;
the pines, definite, given by our hands to replicate
    for our pictures our touch

gentle against the wood. Or we to sunlight
        before their action and increasing
the depth of our excitement with each increase
        of red light by sunlight falling
upon the wood. It was hard to feel: hands,
        red light, projection of ourselves
into the pines to try sensations of being part.
        Or going outside in the usual way.
Through the door instead of the glass—
        our first action being a revival

of the house around us—stairs, floors, walls
        more wood than green
in their persisting in their arrangement
        despite the lack of our attention
to sustain them. We to air light, pictures,
        what goes active in the wood,
loosed plural again our rooms into bark
        restored by being true
bark, no longer active but holding beneath it
        layers more active than our hands

within it, moving. Ours to fear: brown rings
        as bent, film brown to shade,
the pines unframed by our casting centers
        on their centers as we saw them
in the wood. But we were doing something.
        We shifted limbs to disorder—
frames, points, the pictures vague as branches
        tracing cuts throughout the pines.
We with water would wash them blue to varied
        ground beneath the canopy, to shade

light beneath our hands; we internal responding
        to capture would blue-light
capture with our care for those small branches
        then easily cut through by contemplation
of what could be sharper in the pictures. Hands,
        rings—it grew later. And the canopy
must be black and rapid with height against the far
        red of that light that would pass
as through veins to clear the vessels of some weight,
        some dangerous stay within

the stem stuck upright so forward and rigid
        as if in fear of what yet
would move it. We would move it. We redder
        beneath than within would need
that blue going darker as we needed air
        against our cuts to cure
the pictures of the pines, cracks, sun-flecks
        over our seeing not blue light
housing the window formed by the frame
        we formed to frame it, but instead

those hands beside us, still worried. Still
        indoors. Our senses from
outside would be to one another as eyes apart
        but looking right up close
at their apartness and widening, not at the trees
        as they saw them beneath
the glass, but at the pines as we held them fast
        to black, collecting evening meanings
inside us, we having what we believed must be
        our own peculiar way of feeling,

if only a little, those feelings secondary to what our
    senses could yield us in pictures
exposed through blue light to profusion, the inexhaustible
    growing and shrinking back again
of the cracks we fingered to prove it. We knew
    what would not follow our shins
pushing gaps through the grass. Engagement,
    active, of what we called ours
went still redder than the white of those clouds
    absorbing light and composed of parts—

actually separate, actually working in opposition
    to one another, creating tension
between us and that separateness we would not
    call ours: sun through thin clouds,
how we stood in the pictures, that we stood
    for the pictures. But not to repair.
We in our reaching state could not sustain
    the pressure of some clumsy play
at seaming the narrow bands grooved to peel
    open over our wrists. And the glass

made it different from how we remembered.
    We in that room were more
than two receiving; we had within the white
    flat real things and we felt adequate
together protecting them. Our hands made burdens
    of our patience, trailing damp rings
around the room. There was no colored light
    to fall on the wood. It was precious
to us; the inward frames of our hands made square
    houses to remind us of things

that happen in houses—collection, arrangement—
    we would lean to look in.
But those other people—we must appear to them
    unmoved. We must put up with them
in the regular ways. They would have our mystery
    lined to limit what might be
awe at the possibility of trying what we were trying
    though we would never say
we were trying; we were passive even in our action
    (film, hands, the pines sounding rings)

    together making tools of our detachment, our stayed
            leaning to feel it, more. The frames:
limbs fit together to measure need in triangles
            of blue light. It meant our necks
arched out of vertical, compression; it meant
            need in triangles of blue light.
We would give our knees bent to joint floors
            gone wooden in the pictures
produced in the dark to make visible the postures
            of our minds less joint now

than those boards bearing enlargement
            on our papers put in contact
with the glass. And when we said we wanted
            to walk through the black
that made the pines an end around the house,
            we meant I did. I would stand
behind the glass making evening mean the pines
            black through blue light, which is
twilight in early summer when I pictured you
            sleeping soundly in that room

and me finding the pines to be black shapes
        made of cardboard glued
upright in boxes that opened loudly beneath
        my hands. We would not have it;
you as I'd make you—an other, not so exposed—
        would picture me sleeping
soundly in that room and you would watch the pines
        inching closer to the edge
which was to you the glass you pressed against
        your hands drying more in our room

than in the pictures where they drew dark limbs
        out for cutting. The minor
transformations of those hacked branches within
        each frame seemed to seek
increasingly to make themselves new, to build
        into their arrangements a reference
to what we could call true: hands, lines, that it grew
        cooler as the light went bluer or
that we were too warm in that room with its walls
        through which we could not pass.

That touching bark, no longer green, grew
        to wooden around us as our cuts
grew to dry within the pines acting lately
        like shadows on the window
framing hours. We had two ways of making
        words for one another, both ours.
That the cut ends of the branches scraped shapes
        against the glass; it meant need
in pieces of good sky produced in the dark
        and perfectly visible.

Notes

"Like Lamps along the Shoreline" draws inspiration for its title from Virginia Woolf's "The Moment: Summer's Night," in *The Moment and Other Essays,* edited by Leonard Woolf (Harcourt Brace, 1948).

Portions of "Lock, Means" are indebted to Stephen C. Pepper's 1937 article "A Convergence Theory of Similarity," in *The Philosophical Review* 46, number 6: 596–608.

Several poems in the book adapt language from the *Oxford English Dictionary,* particularly its definitions of the words "pattern," "hand," and "moment."

Acknowledgments

Sincere thanks to the editors who first published versions of these poems: an excerpt of "We Meant I Did" appeared in *American Letters & Commentary*; "Limbs Move Wind In" appeared in *At Length*; "Box, Beside" and "Drawer, in Hopes" appeared in *Chicago Review*; the sequences titled "Lock, Means" and "We Meant I Did" were published in a chapbook by Dancing Girl Press; "Green State" appeared in *DIAGRAM*; and "As transparent bodies suffer" appeared in a chapbook published by Hand Held Editions.

I am deeply grateful to my generous teachers, especially Timothy Donnelly, Stephen Fredman, Sidney Goldfarb, Elizabeth Robinson, and Marjorie Welish, for their inspiration and guidance; to my insightful readers at Columbia for their care with my work; to Dan Beachy-Quick for the great compliment of his selection of this manuscript; and to the folks at Tupelo Press for their dedication to crafting beautiful books. I also owe special thanks to my mother and father for their boundless support, as well as to my amazing husband and daughters for whole calendars full of festival days.

Other Books from Tupelo Press

Fasting for Ramadan: Notes from a Spiritual Practice (memoir), Kazim Ali
Fountain and Furnace (poems), Hadara Bar-Nadav
Another English: Anglophone Poems from Around the World (anthology),
   edited by Catherine Barnett and Tiphanie Yanique
Pulp Sonnets (poems, with drawings by Amin Mansouri), Tony Barnstone
Moonbook and Sunbook (poems), Willis Barnstone
gentlessness (poems), Dan Beachy-Quick
One Hundred Hungers (poems), Lauren Camp
New Cathay: Contemporary Chinese Poetry (anthology), edited by Ming Di
Calazaza's Delicious Dereliction (poems) Suzanne Dracius, translated by
   Nancy Naomi Carlson
Gossip and Metaphysics: Russian Modernist Poetry and Prose (anthology), edited by
   Katie Farris, Ilya Kaminsky, and Valzhyna Mort
The Posthumous Affair (novel), James Friel
Entwined: Three Lyric Sequences (poems), Carol Frost
Poverty Creek Journal (lyric memoir), Thomas Gardner
The Good Dark (poems), Annie Guthrie
The Faulkes Chronicle (novel), David Huddle
Darktown Follies (poems), Amaud Jamaul Johnson
A God in the House: Poets Talk About Faith (interviews), edited by Ilya Kaminsky
   and Katherine Towler
Boat (poems), Christopher Merrill
Lucky Fish (poems), Aimee Nezhukumatathil
The Infant Scholar (poems), Kathy Nilsson
Weston's Unsent Letters to Modotti (poems), Chad Parmenter
Ex-Voto (poems), Adélia Prado, translated by Ellen Doré Watson
Mistaking Each Other for Ghosts (poems), Lawrence Raab
Intimate: An American Family Photo Album (hybrid memoir), Paisley Rekdal
Thrill-Bent (novel), Jan Richman
The Book of Stones and Angels (poems), Harold Schweizer
Cream of Kohlrabi (stories), Floyd Skloot
The Perfect Life (lyric essays), Peter Stitt
Soldier On (poems), Gale Marie Thompson
Swallowing the Sea (essays), Lee Upton
Lantern Puzzle (poems), Ye Chun

See our complete list at www.tupelopress.org